Contents

What is the environment?

The environment is the world
all around us.

We need to care for
the environment.

What is reusing?

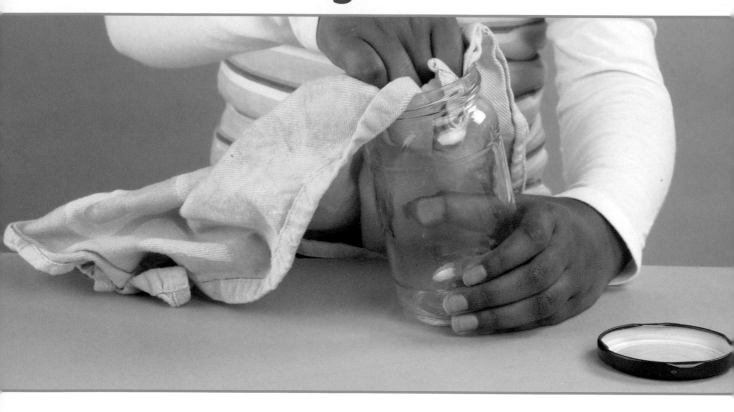

Reusing is using
old things again.

When we reuse things,
we make less rubbish.
We are helping the environment.

When we reuse boxes,
we are saving cardboard.

We are helping the environment.

When we reuse paper,
we are saving paper.
We are helping the environment.

What is recycling?

glass bottles

Recycling is making new things
from old things.

When we recycle things,
we are not wasting them.
We are helping the environment.

glass

We use glass for many things.

When we recycle glass,
we are not wasting glass.
We are helping the environment.

We use plastic for many things.

When we recycle plastic,
we are not wasting plastic.
We are helping the environment. 15

We use paper for many things.

When we recycle paper,
we are not wasting paper.
We are helping the environment.

We use metal for many things.

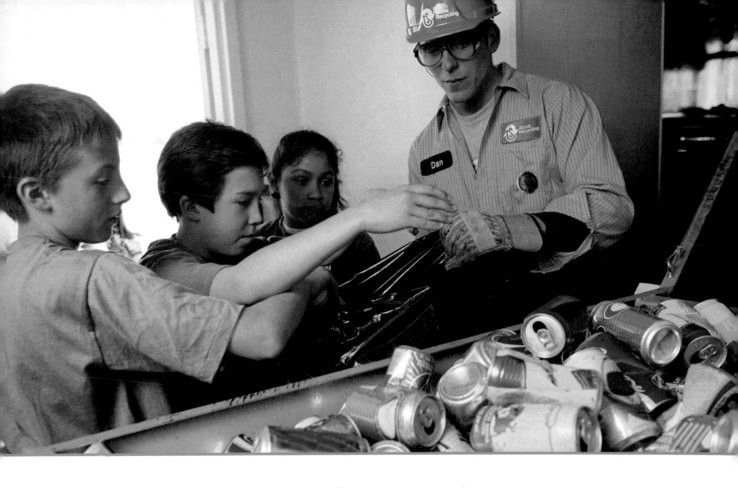

When we recycle metal,
we are not wasting metal.
We are helping the environment.

reuse

recycle

We can reuse and recycle every day.

We can help the environment.

How are they helping?

How are these people reusing things?

Answer on p. 24

Picture glossary

 **environment** the world around us

 **recycle** make old things into new things

 **reuse** use again

Index

Answer to question on p.22: These people are buying old things so that they can use them again.

Note to Parents and Teachers

Before reading

Talk to children about reusing and recycling. Explain how it helps the environment. Show them a sock that is too small for them to wear. What suggestions can they come up with for reusing it? For example, using it as stuffing for a soft toy or making a sock puppet. Ask children to think about things that they can recycle, such as drink cans and paper.

After reading

• Make a 'catcher' from an old plastic milk bottle. Wash the bottle thoroughly. Cut off the bottom of the bottle and then cut a U shape under the handle. (NB Don't cut into the handle itself.) Decorate the catcher with coloured sticky tape. In the playground challenge pairs of children to see how many 'catches' they can do.

• Ask children to bring in any material that can be reused to make something new (used foil, egg boxes, newspaper, old wool, fabric, etc.). Draw a very large outline of an animal, such as a lion or a dinosaur. Help children cut up some of the material and decide where to place it on the outline to make a collage picture.

• Sing a recycling song to the tune of 'London Bridge is Falling Down'. For example, 'We recycle newspapers, newspapers, newspapers. We recycle newspapers to save our planet.' Sing other verses about plastic bottles, empty cans, and so on.